SRA
OPEN COURT READING

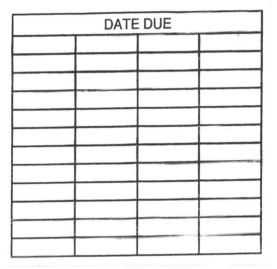

DATE DUE			

T   on

A Division of The McGraw·Hill Companies

Columbus, Ohio

www.sra4kids.com

SRA/McGraw-Hill

A Division of The McGraw·Hill Companies

Send all inquiries to:
SRA/McGraw-Hill
8787 Orion Place
Columbus, OH 43240-4027

Printed in the United States of America.

ISBN 0-07-569572-3

2 3 4 5 6 7 8 9 QPD 07 06 05 04 03 02

Table of Contents

Unit 4 Survival

Unit 5 Communication

Unit 6 A Changing America

Knowledge About Risks and Consequences

- This is what I know about taking risks and the consequences of taking risks before reading the unit.

Answers will vary.

_____

_____

_____

_____

_____

- These are some things about risks and consequences that I would like to talk about, investigate, and understand better.

Answers will vary.

_____

_____

_____

_____

_____

Reminder: I should read this page again when I get to the end of the unit to see how much I have learned about risks and consequences.

UNIT 1 Risks and Consequences

Recording Concept Information

As I read each selection, I learned these facts about risks and consequences.

- "Mrs. Frisby and the Crow" by Robert C. O'Brien
Answers will vary.

_____

_____

_____

_____

_____

_____

_____

_____

- "Toto" by Marietta D. Moskin
Answers will vary.

_____

_____

_____

_____

_____

_____

_____

_____

- "Sarah, Plain and Tall" by Patricia MacLachlan
  Answers will vary.

- "Escape" by E. B. White
  Answers will vary.

- "Mae Jemison: Space Scientist" by Gail Sakurai

Answers will vary.

_____

_____

_____

_____

_____

_____

_____

_____

- "Two Tickets to Freedom" by Florence B. Freedman

Answers will vary.

_____

_____

_____

_____

_____

_____

_____

_____

• "Daedalus and Icarus" by Geraldine McCaughrean

Answers will vary.

UNIT 1 Risks and Consequences

Project Planning

Use the calendar to help schedule your investigation on Risks and Consequences. Fill in the dates. Make sure that you mark any days you know you will not be able to work on your investigation. Then choose the date on which you will start

Sunday	Monday	Tuesday	Wednesday

and the date on which you hope to finish. You may also find it helpful to mark the dates by which you hope to complete each part of the investigation. Record what you accomplish each day.

Thursday	Friday	Saturday

Name _____ Date _____

Generating Questions to Investigate

What other questions about risks and consequences would you like to learn more about? Write them here.

Answers will vary.

_____

_____

_____

_____

Now think about these questions. Are there people whom you admire because they take risks? Who are they? What risks have they taken?

Person	Risk
Answers will vary.	

Below are more questions to think about:
- Does everyone agree on what a risk is?
- Do you have to be a certain kind of person to take risks?
- Can you do things to make a risk less risky?

Think of ways in which you could find anwers to these questions. Write them here.

Answers will vary.

_____

_____

_____

Have you come up with something that you would like to investigate? Write your questions or ideas at the top of this page.

Choosing Appropriate Sources

Make a list of topics that you want to learn more about from "Mrs. Frisby and the Crow." Possible topics may investigate the author of the story or the relationship between an animal and its prey.

Think of topics you would like to learn more about. Write three topics here. **Possible answers shown.**

The relationship between cats and mice;

the difference between a fantasy story and

a biography; the illustrator, Barbara Lanza

Choose the topic you would most like to learn about.
Answers will vary.

There are many sources you can use to investigate your favorite topic.

Encyclopedia	Internet
Books	Videotapes
Magazines	Television
Newspapers	Interviews
Dictionary	Pamphlets and brochures

Choose two sources and answer the following questions.

First Source: ___ **Answers will vary.** _____

• What type of information does this source contain?

_____

_____

_____

• What might you learn from this source about your topic?

_____

_____

_____

• Find an example of this source in a library or in your
classroom that you can use in your investigation.
Write the title of the source.

_____

_____

Second Source: **Answers will vary.**

• What type of information does this source contain?

_____

_____

_____

• What might you learn from this source about your topic?

_____

_____

_____

• Find an example of this source in a library or in your
classroom that you can use in your investigation.
Write the title of the source.

_____

_____

Taking Notes

Taking notes means writing down information from investigation sources. Good notes contain key phrases and short sentences that sum up important facts and ideas. When taking notes, follow these guidelines:

- Create subject headings and use them to organize your notes.
- Include only the most important information on the topic.
- Write notes in your own words.
- Keep your notes short. Use abbreviations and key phrases that you will recognize.

Write the name of your topic for your investigation. Look through some of the resources you have chosen for your investigation, such as an almanac or magazine. Select two and write notes from these resources. Create subheadings for your notes to help you organize and classify different types of information.

The title of my topic is: **Answers will vary.** _____

1. Resource title:

_____

_____

Notes:

_____

_____

_____

_____

_____

2. Resource title:

_____

_____

Notes:

_____

_____

_____

_____

_____

_____

_____

_____

_____

_____

_____

_____

_____

_____

_____

_____

_____

Framing Questions to Find Information

"Sarah, Plain and Tall" includes topics such as living on the prairie and family. Based on the story, fill in the chart with questions about four topics you would like to investigate. Write one question for each topic. Then find answers to your questions either by rereading the selection or by investigating the information in another source. **Possible answers are shown.**

Questions About a Topic	Information I Found
1. **How was food cooked in past times?**	**From the story I learned that a wood-burning stove was used.**
2. **What were horses used for in past times?**	**From the story I learned that they were used for transportation.** **I also learned from the encyclopedia that they were used for hauling equipment.**

Questions About a Topic	Information I Found
3.	
4.	

Using the Dictionary

Often you will find new words when you are investigating a topic. A dictionary can help you understand new words that you find in your reading and help you use them correctly in your writing. Look through "Escape" for three words that are unfamiliar to you. Write these words and their definitions, including synonyms and antonyms, in the chart below.

Possible answers shown.

Word	Definition (including synonyms and antonyms)
1. **comfortable**	At ease synonym: relaxed antonym: tense
2. **awful**	Causing fear or dread. synonym: terrible antonym: lovely
3.	

- How does knowing the meaning of these words help your understanding of the story?

Answers will vary.

- How can you use these words in your investigation?

Answers will vary.

Name _____ Date _____

Risks and Heroes

Take a minute to investigate your ideas about heroes and heroism. What does a person have to do to be considered a hero?

Answers will vary.

_____

_____

_____

Name three persons that you consider heroes. Why are they heroes?

	Person	**Reason**
1.	_____	_____
2.	_____	_____
3.	_____	_____

Why do you think heroes are so important to us? What effect do they have on us?

_____

_____

_____

Work with your classmates to create a Heroes Hall of Fame in your classroom. Who would you like to see in the Hall of Fame? Write your ideas here.

_____

_____

_____

UNIT I **Risks and Consequences**

Using a Thesaurus

Authors use a thesaurus to help them find the best word to say what they mean. Choose six words from a piece of writing in your *Writing Folder* that you could change to make the sentences more interesting or exact. Use a thesaurus to find a synonym for each word.

Words from my selection: Synonyms:

Answers will vary.
_____   _____

_____   _____

_____   _____

_____   _____

_____   _____

Rewrite the sentences with the synonyms in place. Make sure that the sentences have the same meaning as before.

_____

_____

_____

_____

_____

_____

_____

_____

_____

Using a thesaurus, replace the underlined words without changing the meaning of the sentence. **Answers will vary.**

• The <u>proud</u> and <u>noble</u> knight rode across the field on his <u>powerful</u> steed.

_____

_____

What kind of person is the knight?

_____

_____

• Their house was <u>humble</u> and <u>bare</u> of any <u>luxurious</u> furniture.

_____

_____

What kind of house do they live in?

_____

_____

• The room was <u>colorful</u> and <u>bright</u>.

_____

_____

What other words would you use to describe the house?

_____

_____

Name _____ Date _____

Risks and Freedom

Ellen and William Craft were willing to risk everything to escape to freedom. Every year thousands of people leave behind their homes, their countries, and everything they know to come to the United States to begin new lives.
- Why are they willing to do this?
- What might their lives have been like at home?
- What might they be expecting life in the United States to be like?

Talk with classmates, and try to answer these questions. Write your ideas here.

Answers will vary.

_____

_____

_____

_____

What risks do these new Americans face? Why can it be hard—and sometimes frightening—to start a new life in the United States?

_____

_____

_____

_____

Why do you think freedom is so important to people? Why is it important to you? Write your thoughts here.

_____

_____

_____

Name _____ Date _____

Maps and Atlases

Map A

Map B

Write five questions about either Map A or Map B. Give your questions to a classmate. When your classmate has finished answering them, discuss the questions. Share how maps could be useful in your research project for this or other units.

1. **Answers will vary.** _____

_____

2. _____

_____

3. _____

_____

4. _____

_____

5. _____

_____

UNIT 1 Risks and Consequences

Asking Additional Questions

   In this unit, you have investigated an aspect of the theme Risks and Consequences. It is important to remember that research is an ongoing process that generates new ideas, questions, and wonderings. Are there any additional questions you would like to investigate about risks and consequences? Did any of the stories you read about risks and consequences generate new questions? In the spaces below, list any further questions about risks and consequences that you would like to investigate.

Additional questions I would like to investigate:

Answers will vary.

_____

_____

_____

_____

_____

Think of ways in which you could find answers to these questions. Write them here.

Answers will vary.

_____

_____

_____

_____

_____

_____

Unit Wrap-Up

- How do you feel about this unit?

  ☐ I enjoyed it very much.   ☐ I liked it.

  ☐ I liked some of it.   ☐ I didn't like it.

- How would you rate the difficulty of the unit?

  ☐ easy   ☐ medium   ☐ hard

- How would you rate your performance during this unit?

  ☐ I learned a lot about risks and consequences.

  ☐ I learned some new things about risks
     and consequences.

  ☐ I didn't learn much about risks and consequences.

- Explain your last answer.

  Answers will vary.

  _____

  _____

  _____

- What was the most interesting thing that you learned about
  risks and consequences?

  Answers will vary.

  _____

  _____

  _____

- What did you learn about risks and consequences that you hadn't known before?

  Answers will vary.

  _____

  _____

  _____

- What did you learn about yourself as a learner?

  Answers will vary.

  _____

  _____

  _____

- What do you need to work on as a learner?

  Answers will vary.

  _____

  _____

  _____

- What resources (books, films, magazines, interviews, other) did you use on your own during this unit? Which of these were the most helpful? Why?

  Answers will vary.

  _____

  _____

  _____

Knowledge About Business

• This is what I know about business before reading the unit.
Answers will vary.

_____

_____

_____

_____

_____

• These are some things I would like to know about business.
Answers will vary.

_____

_____

_____

_____

_____

Reminder: I should read this page again when I get to
the end of the unit to see how much I have learned about
business.

UNIT 2 Dollars and Sense

Recording Concept Information

As I read each selection, I learned these new facts about business.

- "Starting a Business" by Arlene Erlbach
  Answers will vary.
  _____

  _____

  _____

  _____

  _____

  _____

  _____

  _____

  _____

- "Henry Wells and William G. Fargo" by Edward F. Dolan, Jr.
  Answers will vary.
  _____

  _____

  _____

  _____

  _____

  _____

  _____

- "Elias Sifuentes, Restaurateur" by Neil Johnson

   Answers will vary.

   _____

   _____

   _____

   _____

   _____

   _____

   _____

- "Food from the 'Hood" by Marlene Targ Brill

   Answers will vary.

   _____

   _____

   _____

   _____

   _____

   _____

   _____

   _____

- "Business Is Looking Up" by Barbara Aiello and Jeffrey Shulman

Answers will vary.

_____

_____

_____

_____

_____

_____

_____

- "Salt" by Harve Zemach

Answers will vary.

_____

_____

_____

_____

_____

_____

_____

- "The Milkmaid and Her Pail" by Aesop

Answers will vary.

_____

_____

_____

_____

_____

_____

_____

_____

_____

_____

_____

_____

Name _____ Date _____

Project Planning

Use the calendar to help schedule your investigation on business. Fill in the dates. Make sure that you mark any days you know you will not be able to work on your investigation. Then choose the date on which you will start and the date on

Sunday	Monday	Tuesday	Wednesday

which you hope to finish. You may also find it helpful to mark the dates by which you hope to complete each part of the investigation. Record what you accomplish each day.

Thursday	Friday	Saturday

UNIT 2 Dollars and Sense

Encyclopedias and Other Print Media

Use a variety of print media when you investigate a topic. Here are some examples of different types of print media.

- An **encyclopedia** is a set of books with articles on almost everything. The articles are listed in alphabetical order by subject.
- An **atlas** is a book of maps.
- An **almanac** is a single reference book that has facts and summaries of information. An almanac is published yearly.
- **Newspapers** are a daily source of information about current events.
- **Magazines** contain a weekly, monthly, or quarterly collection of news or information on general or specific topics.

Select a favorite fruit or vegetable. If you do not have a favorite fruit or vegetable, choose any one you would like to know more about. Find information about it in each source listed below.

Your favorite fruit or vegetable: __**Answers will vary.**_____

1. Encyclopedia

   Title: _____

   Page(s): _____ Volume number: _____

   Information I found: _____

   _____

   _____

   _____

   _____

   _____

2. Almanac

Title: _____ Page(s): _____

Information I found: _____

_____

_____

_____

3. Magazine

Title: _____ Date: _____

Article title: _____

Written by: _____ Page(s): _____

Information I found: _____

_____

_____

_____

4. Newspaper

Title: _____ Date: _____

Article title: _____

Written by: _____ Page(s): _____

Information I found: _____

_____

_____

_____

Name _____ Date _____

Business Problems and Solutions

Most businesses experience problems, such as how to get people to buy their goods and services. The owners need to work out solutions. Think about the two selections you have read in this unit. In the boxes below, write the problems and solutions presented in the stories. **Answers will vary.**

Starting a Business

Problem		**Solution**
	→	

Henry Wells and William G. Fargo

Problem		**Solution**
	→	

Name _____ Date _____

Conjecture Phase

Our problem:
Answers will vary.

_____

_____

_____

_____

_____

_____

Conjecture (my first theory or explanation):

_____

_____

_____

_____

_____

_____

_____

   As you collect information, your conjecture will change.
Return to this page to record your new theories or
explanations about your investigation.

UNIT 2 Dollars and Sense

Parts of a Book

Understanding the parts of a book will help you find information faster because you will know where to look. Some books, but not all, have these parts.

These pages are at the front of many books.
- The **title page** gives the title of the book, the names of the author or editor and the illustrator, and the name of the publisher.
- The **copyright page** gives the publisher's name and the place and year the book was published.
- The **table of contents** lists, in numerical order, the units, chapters, or stories in the book with the page number on which each item begins.

These pages are at the back of many books.
- The **index** is an alphabetical list in the back of the book of important names and subjects and the pages on which they appear.
- The **bibliography** is a list of books, newspapers, magazines, and other resources that the author used for information.
- The **glossary** is an alphabetical list of special words used in the book and their definitions.

Use books from the library or your classroom to answer these questions.

1. Complete the following about a fiction book that contains this information.

   Title: **Answers will vary.** _____

   Author: _____

   Illustrator: _____

   Copyright date: _____

Where can you find the name of the publisher? **title and copyright pages**

Where can you find a list of the units and chapter titles in a book? **table of contents**

2. Complete the following about a nonfiction book that contains this information

Title: **Answers will vary.** _____

Copyright date: _____

Author(s) or Editor(s): _____

Illustrator or Photographer: _____

What is the title of the first chapter? _____

The first chapter begins on which page? _____

Based on the chapter title, what is Chapter 1 about? _____

_____

These four words and page numbers are listed in the index.

_____

_____

_____

These four words and their meanings are from the glossary.

_____

_____

_____

UNIT 2 Dollars and Sense

Investigation Plan

Think about your investigation based on what you know about business. Make a plan for your group's investigation. Decide what information needs to be gathered by each group member. Write the group members' names and assignments in the chart.

Group Members	Main Jobs
Answers will vary.	

Interviewing

Interviewing is a way to gather information, an opinion, or a story from one person's point of view. Remember to follow these rules:

- Always ask permission to interview the person. Make sure the person knows how much time you will need for the interview.
- Make up questions that will help you get the information you need. Use questions that begin with *who*, *what*, *when*, *where*, or *why*.
- Write your questions in an organized order, with space after each one for taking notes.
- Speak clearly and be polite.
- Read over your notes immediately after you leave the interview, while the conversation is still fresh in your mind.
- If you plan to record the interview with a tape recorder or a videotape recorder, ask the person's permission first.

Make a list of people you might like to interview.

Answers will vary.

_____

_____

_____

_____

Write how interviews might be useful in your investigation.

Answers will vary.

_____

_____

_____

_____

Interviewing *(continued)*

What questions will you ask the person you interview?
What do you especially want to know? Write some questions
that you will ask the person you interview. Make sure you do
not ask any questions that can be answered with a simple
"yes" or "no." Discuss these questions with your classmates.

1. **Answers will vary.**
   _____

2. _____
   _____

3. _____
   _____

4. _____
   _____

5. _____
   _____

Write what you learned from the interview.

Answers will vary.
_____

_____

_____

_____

_____

_____

_____

Gathering Information

Before you begin to gather information, decide on a topic
to research for your investigation.

- My group's topic:
  Answers will vary.
  _____

  _____

- Information I need to find or figure out about my topic:
  Answers will vary.
  _____

  _____

  _____

  _____

Complete the chart below to help you decide which sources
will be useful.

Sources	Useful?	How?
Encyclopedias		
Books		
Magazines		
Newspapers		
Videotapes, filmstrips, etc.		
Television		
Interviews, observations		
Museums		
Other		

UNIT 2 Dollars and Sense

Presenting Information

How might you present the information that you found to your classmates? You could make a poster or chart, build a tabletop model, or even create a videotape.

• Write information you found on your topic.

Answers will vary.

_____

_____

_____

_____

_____

_____

_____

• List some of the ways you might present your information.

Answers will vary.

_____

_____

_____

_____

_____

_____

_____

Name _____   Date _____

Summarizing and Organizing Information

Summarizing will help you organize information and remember what you have read. When you write a summary, look for the main ideas and important details, and use your own words to tell what happens in the story. Select a story from Unit 2. Write the title on the line below. Summarize the story by filling in the flow chart. Write the main ideas and important details from the story in your own words.

Title: _____

How does the story begin?
Answers will vary.
_____

↓

What happens next?
_____
_____

↓

What happens after that?
_____
_____

↓

How does the story end?
_____
_____

Choose a well-known book or movie, but do not put the title of it on the flow chart. Summarize the story on the flow chart. Then, exchange papers with a partner. Guess the title of the book or movie on your partner's flow chart. Write it on the line below.

How does the story begin?

Answers will vary.

_____

_____

↓

What happens next?

_____

_____

↓

What happens after that?

_____

_____

↓

How does the story end?

_____

_____

Can you guess the title? Write it here.

_____

Title guessed by (name): _____

Asking Additional Questions

Complete this chart after each presentation to help you evaluate the questions you and your classmates researched.

Research Question	How It Contributed to My Knowledge of Business	New Questions Raised
Information will vary.		

Research Question	How It Contributed to My Knowledge of Business	New Questions Raised

Name _____ Date _____

Reasons and Ideas

People start businesses for many different reasons, and business ideas come from many sources. Think about your business plan for the investigation. What are your reasons for choosing your business? Where did your ideas about your business come from? A book from the library? A magazine article? Write your reasons and sources for ideas in the boxes below. If you did not create a business plan for the investigation, use any business idea that you may have.

Reasons

Answers will vary.
_____
_____
_____
_____
_____

Sources for Ideas

Answers will vary.
_____
_____
_____
_____
_____

UNIT 2 Dollars and Sense

Organizing Information in Charts

A chart is a good way to organize similar information about a topic.

• A chart has a title that tells what the chart is about.
• Row headings are on the left side of the chart.
• Column headings are across the top of the chart and describe the information given about each item.

Using the information on page 53, fill in the chart below.

Steel

Kind	Content	Uses
Carbon	**Contains less than 1 percent carbon**	**Building beams, automobile bodies, cans, and kitchen appliances**
Alloy steel	**Contains some carbon and other elements**	**Used in specialty products that require toughness**
Stainless steel	**12 to 30 percent chromium**	**Pots and pans, hospital equipment, razor blades, knives, and tableware**
Tool steel	**Carbon or alloy steel**	**Metalworking tools**

Kinds of Steel

The metal called steel is an alloy, or mixture, of the element iron with other elements, such as manganese, nickel, aluminum, chromium, and copper. Each element improves the steel. Manganese makes steel harder. Nickel improves its ability to withstand very low temperatures.

There are four basic varieties of steel. Carbon steel is the most common. It contains less than 1 percent carbon. It is widely used in building beams, automobile bodies, cans, and kitchen appliances.

Alloy steel contains some carbon and other elements that improve the steel by making it resistant to rust, heat, cold, or hard wear. It is used in specialty products that require toughness.

Stainless steel is the most resistant to rusting because it contains from 12 to 30 percent chromium. It is used to make pots and pans, hospital equipment, razor blades, knives, and other tableware.

Tool steel is made very hard by tempering—that is, heating and quickly cooling—carbon or alloy steel. It is used to make metalworking tools.

UNIT 2 Dollars and Sense

Unit Wrap-Up

- How do you feel about this unit?

  ☐ I enjoyed it very much.   ☐ I liked it.

  ☐ I liked some of it.   ☐ I didn't like it.

- How would you rate the difficulty of the unit?

  ☐ easy   ☐ medium   ☐ hard

- How would you rate your performance during this unit?

  ☐ I learned a lot about business.

  ☐ I learned some new things about business.

  ☐ I didn't learn much about business.

- Explain your last answer.

  Answers will vary.

  _____

  _____

  _____

- What was the most interesting thing that you learned about business?

  Answers will vary.

  _____

  _____

  _____

- What did you learn about business that you hadn't known before?

  Answers will vary.

  _____

  _____

  _____

- What did you learn about yourself as a learner?

  Answers will vary.

  _____

  _____

  _____

- What do you need to work on as a learner?

  Answers will vary.

  _____

  _____

  _____

- What resources (books, films, magazines, interviews, other) did you use on your own during this unit? Which of these were the most helpful? Why?

  Answers will vary.

  _____

  _____

  _____

Name _____ Date _____

Knowledge About Medicine

- This is what I know about medicine before reading the unit.
  Answers will vary.

_____

_____

_____

_____

_____

_____

_____

- These are some things I would like to know about medicine.
  Answers will vary.

_____

_____

_____

_____

_____

_____

_____

Reminder: I should read this page again when I get to the
end of the unit to see how much I have learned about medicine.

Name _____ Date _____

Recording Concept Information

As I read each selection, I learned these new facts about medicine.

- "Medicine: Past and Present" by André W. Carus
  Answers will vary.

_____

_____

_____

_____

_____

_____

- "Sewed Up His Heart" by Lillie Patterson
  Answers will vary.

_____

_____

_____

_____

_____

_____

_____

_____

- "The Bridge Dancers" by Carol Saller
  Answers will vary.

  _____

  _____

  _____

  _____

  _____

- "Emily's Hands-On Science Experiment" by Hugh Westrup
  Answers will vary.

  _____

  _____

  _____

  _____

  _____

- "The New Doctor" by Paula G. Paul
  Answers will vary.

  _____

  _____

  _____

  _____

  _____

  _____

  _____

  _____

- "The Story of Susan La Flesche Picotte"
  by Marion Marsh Brown
  Answers will vary.

_____

_____

_____

_____

_____

_____

_____

- "Shadow of a Bull" by Maia Wojciechowska
  Answers will vary.

_____

_____

_____

_____

_____

_____

_____

_____

UNIT 3 From Mystery to Medicine

Project Planning

Use the calendar to help schedule your investigation on From Mystery to Medicine. Fill in the dates. Make sure that you mark any days you know you will not be able to work on your investigation. Then choose the date on which you will

Sunday	Monday	Tuesday	Wednesday

start and the date on which you hope to finish. You may also find it helpful to mark the dates by which you hope to complete each part of the investigation. Record what you accomplish each day.

Thursday	Friday	Saturday

UNIT 3 From Mystery to Medicine

People in Medicine

Many people have contributed to the field of medicine. In this unit, you will read about some of these people and the work they did. Some of the people you will read about are listed in the chart below. As you read the stories in this unit, complete the chart by writing the major contributions of each person you have read about.

Are there other people in medicine you would like to know about? Look through other resources in your classroom or library, such as magazines or nonfiction books. Add to your chart other interesting people in medicine and their contributions. Share your findings with your classmates and think about how you can use this information in your investigation.

Person	Contribution
William Harvey	**discovered that blood circulates through the bodies of humans and animals**
Anton van Leeuwenhoek	**used a powerful microscope to discover microbes, or "tiny animals," swimming in pond water**
Edward Jenner	**discovered a way of preventing smallpox**

Person	Contribution
Louis Pasteur	**invented the process known as pasteurization, in which heat is used to kill bacteria**
Alexander Fleming	**discovered penicillin, a type of mold that kills bacteria**
Susan La Flesche Picotte	**the first female Native American doctor in the United States**
Daniel Hale Williams	**performed the first successful heart surgery**

UNIT 3 From Mystery to Medicine

Time Lines

A time line can help you understand when important events occurred and the order in which they happened. A time line may cover any length of time, from the lifetime of a person to a historical period of hundreds or thousands of years.

Important Events in Medicine

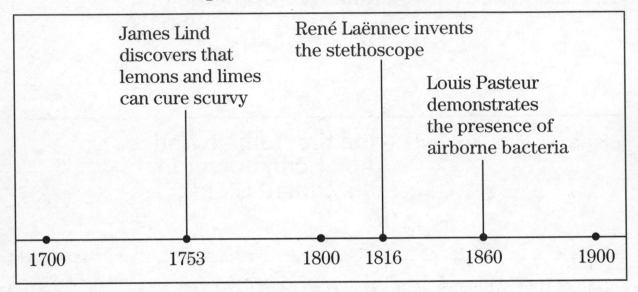

Here are some things to remember about time lines.
- Each dot on the line represents a date.
- Each dot represents at least one event.
- A time line usually has a title that indicates the type of information that is shown on the line.
- Events are listed on the time line from left to right in the order of occurrence. The earliest event appears at the far left.
- A time line can be made for any set of events. However, time lines usually show meaningful relationships between events.
- Record only important events on a time line. Avoid minor details and unimportant events.

What important school events have happened since the first day of school? Make a time line of these events from the first day of school to today. Begin by listing four important events and the dates of these events in the spaces below. Then put the dates and a brief description of each event on the time line in the box.

1. **Answers will vary.** _____

2. _____

3. _____

4. _____

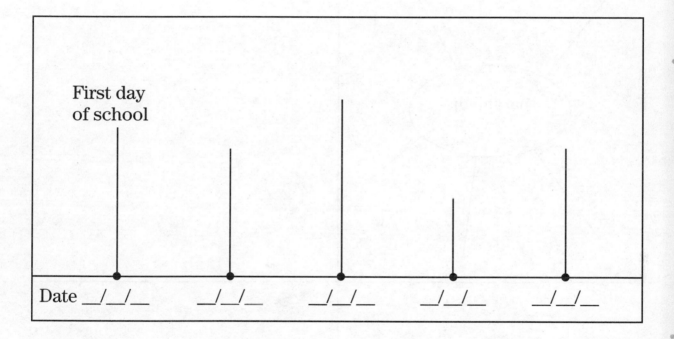

First day
of school

Date __/__/__   __/__/__   __/__/__   __/__/__   __/__/__

How might you use a time line during your investigation?
Answers will vary. _____

_____

_____

_____

_____

Name _____ Date

Careers in Medicine

Many specialists work in the medical field: doctors, nurses, surgeons, researchers, X-ray technicians, and paramedics. Find out about different careers in medicine. Complete the first web. Then, make three webs of your own. Write information and words in the webs about three more careers in medicine. **Answers will vary.**

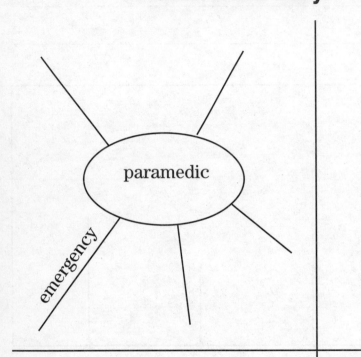

Conjecture Phase

Our problem:
Answers will vary.

_____

_____

_____

_____

_____

_____

Conjecture (my first theory or explanation):
Answers will vary.

_____

_____

_____

_____

_____

_____

_____

   As you collect information, your conjecture will change.
Return to this page to record your new theories or
explanations about your investigation.

Name _____ Date _____

Using Magazines and Other Printed Resources

Magazines, newspapers, and other printed resources have useful, up-to-date information about medicine and other topics.

Find magazines, newspapers, or other printed resources (such as a newsletter) that have information about the topic you chose for your investigation. Choose three different resources that are about the same topic, such as doctors' opinions about herbal medicine. Write the title of the resource, the title of the article, and the date of the publication. Then, write a brief summary of each article.

1. Resource title: **Answers will vary.** _____

   Title of article: _____ Date: _____

   Summary: _____

   _____

   _____

2. Resource title: _____

   Title of article: _____ Date: _____

   Summary: _____

   _____

   _____

3. Resource title: _____

   Title of article: _____ Date: _____

   Summary: _____

   _____

   _____

Write two paragraphs based on the summaries you wrote. Make sure your paragraphs cover the main topic of the articles you selected. Remember to answer the questions *who*, *what*, *where*, *when*, and *why* as you write about the topic. Write an interesting title for your paragraphs.

Title: **Answers will vary.**

_____

_____

_____

_____

_____

_____

_____

_____

_____

_____

_____

_____

_____

_____

_____

_____

_____

_____

Name _____ Date _____

Cures and Preventions

Doctors use many methods to prevent illnesses and to treat those who are sick or injured. Write the importance of each method listed below. Record any other methods that you know.

Vaccines: __**Answers will vary.**_____

_____

_____

_____

_____

_____

Physicals: _____

_____

_____

_____

_____

_____

Over-the-counter medicines: _____

_____

_____

_____

_____

Surgery: _____

_____

_____

_____

_____

_____

_____

_____

Other methods: _____

_____

_____

_____

_____

_____

_____

_____

_____

UNIT 3 From Mystery to Medicine

Diagrams

A diagram is an illustration of the parts of an object, an arrangement of objects, the steps in a process, or the stages in a cycle. Diagrams clarify written information in a book, magazine, or other resource by providing a picture to help readers see how things work.

Here are the kinds of information diagrams can show.

- They can show how something is put together, such as roller skates.
- They can show how something is arranged, such as furniture in a room.
- Diagrams can also show how something works, such as the hip or elbow joints in the body.
- They can show how to make something, such as a model airplane.
- Diagrams can show what steps make up a process, such as making steel.
- They can also show what stages make up a cycle, such as the life cycle of a frog.

Look at the diagram below.

Parts of an In-Line Skate

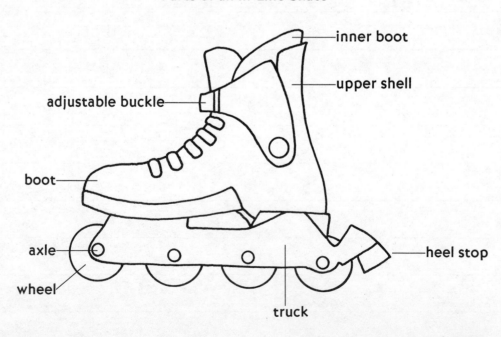

Notice the features of the diagram on page 72. These features are common to most diagrams.

- The **title** of a diagram tells what the diagram shows.
- **Labels** of a diagram tell about the parts of an object or the steps in a process.
- **Lines** lead from each label to a part of an object or one step in a process.
- **Arrows** show the order in which the steps of a process or the stages in a cycle take place. They may also show movement or direction.

Answer the following questions using the diagram of an in-line skate. **Possible answers are shown.**

1. What parts of an in-line skate cover the foot and part of the leg?

inner boot, upper shell, adjustable buckle, boot

2. Can you tell what the truck does by looking at the diagram?

yes _____ What does it do?

It holds the axles of the wheels and the

heel stop.

3. Which part helps you to stop rolling when you skate?

heel stop _____ Describe where that part is located on the

skate. **It is located behind the last wheel in the**

truck and below the upper shell.

Think of how you might use a diagram in your investigation. Write your ideas here.

Answers will vary.

UNIT 3 From Mystery to Medicine

Finding a Topic to Investigate

There are many topics on medicine to choose from, such as famous people in medicine and new discoveries in medical technology. In the spaces below, write one topic you would like to know more about and why. Then, list questions about the topic that you would like to investigate.

• A good topic to investigate:

Answers will vary.

_____

_____

_____

_____

• Why this is an interesting investigation topic:

_____

_____

_____

_____

• Some other questions about this topic:

_____

_____

_____

_____

Medical Technology

Throughout your reading and investigation for this unit, keep track of the different medical items used by doctors and other medical workers. Write a brief summary of how each item is used. Then, draw or paste a picture of each item next to your summary. Look in newspapers and magazines for pictures of these items. Think about how you might use these illustrations or other visual resources in your investigation.

Item	Use	Illustration
microscope	**An instrument with lenses used to view tiny objects**	
stethoscope	**An instrument used to listen to breathing**	
poultice	**A mass of medicinal herbs applied to wounds**	
X-ray machine	**Takes pictures of the bones and organs**	
scalpel	**Used to cut an incision in the flesh for surgery**	

Item	Use	Illustration

Comparing Information Across Sources

Researchers compare a variety of sources when they are looking for information about a topic. To decide which sources are best, the researcher considers the following:
- how old the source is
- the amount of information and details the source has
- whether the information in the source is correct and reliable

Use the topic you chose for your investigation as you compare sources. Think of five sources you might use to find information, such as encyclopedias, nonfiction books, or magazines. Find titles under these sources in your library or classroom. Write the titles and the types of sources in the spaces below.

My topic: **Answers will vary.** _____

1. Title: _____

   Type of source: _____

2. Title: _____

   Type of source: _____

3. Title: _____

   Type of source: _____

4. Title: _____

   Type of source: _____

5. Title: _____

   Type of source: _____

Of the sources you have listed, decide which are the best for your topic. Write two of them in the note cards below and explain why you think they are best.

Title: **Answers will vary.** _____

Type of source: _____

This is one of the best sources because _____

_____

_____

_____

_____

Title: **Answers will vary.** _____

Type of source: _____

This is one of the best sources because _____

_____

_____

_____

_____

Investigation Needs and Plans

Think about your investigation needs and plans. You may need to gather more information and materials for your investigation. Ask questions or talk about any problems you are having with your investigation. Use a separate sheet of paper if you need more space.

My topic: **Answers will vary.**

- Sources I need to add to my research

Sources	Useful?	How?
Encyclopedias		
Books		
Magazines		
Newspapers		
Videotapes, filmstrips, etc.		
Television		
Interviews, observations		
Museums		
Other		

- List two investigation problems you are having. Write possible solutions in the spaces below.

	Problems	Solutions
1.	**Answers will vary.**	
2.		

UNIT 3 From Mystery to Medicine

Unit Wrap-Up

- How do you feel about this unit?

  ☐ I enjoyed it very much.   ☐ I liked it.

  ☐ I liked some of it.   ☐ I didn't like it.

- How would you rate the difficulty of the unit?

  ☐ easy   ☐ medium   ☐ hard

- How would you rate your performance during this unit?

  ☐ I learned a lot about medicine.

  ☐ I learned some new things about medicine.

  ☐ I didn't learn much about medicine.

- Explain your last answer.
  Answers will vary.
  _____
  _____
  _____

- What was the most interesting thing that you learned about medicine?
  Answers will vary.
  _____
  _____
  _____

- What did you learn about medicine that you hadn't known before?

  Answers will vary.

  _____

  _____

  _____

- What did you learn about yourself as a learner?

  Answers will vary.

  _____

  _____

  _____

- What do you need to work on as a learner?

  Answers will vary.

  _____

  _____

  _____

- What resources (books, films, magazines, interviews, other) did you use on your own during this unit? Which of these were the most helpful? Why?

  Answers will vary.

  _____

  _____

  _____

UNIT 4 Survival

Knowledge About Survival

- This is what I know about survival before reading the unit.
  Answers will vary.

_____

_____

_____

_____

_____

_____

_____

- These are some things I would like to know about survival.
  Answers will vary.

_____

_____

_____

_____

_____

_____

_____

Reminder: I should read this page again when I get to the
end of the unit to see how much I have learned about survival.

Recording Concept Information

As I read each selection, I learned these new facts about survival.

- "Island of the Blue Dolphins" by Scott O'Dell
  Answers will vary.
  _____

  _____

  _____

  _____

  _____

  _____

  _____

  _____

- "Arctic Explorer: The Story of Matthew Henson"
  by Jeri Ferris
  Answers will vary.
  _____

  _____

  _____

  _____

  _____

  _____

  _____

  _____

- "McBroom and the Big Wind" by Sid Fleischman
  Answers will vary.

- "The Big Wave" by Pearl S. Buck
  Answers will vary.

- "Anne Frank: The Diary of a Young Girl" by Anne Frank
  Answers will vary.

- "Music and Slavery" by Wiley Blevins
  Answers will vary.

UNIT 4 Survival

Project Planning

Use the calendar to help schedule your investigation on Survival. Fill in the dates. Make sure that you mark any days you know you will not be able to work on your investigation. Then choose the date on which you will start and the date on

Sunday	Monday	Tuesday	Wednesday

which you hope to finish. You may also find it helpful to mark the dates by which you hope to complete each part of the investigation. Record what you accomplish each day.

Thursday	Friday	Saturday

Investigating Online Media

"Island of the Blue Dolphin" is the story of a young girl who is trapped on a deserted island and must overcome loneliness and wild dogs in order to survive. Think of some other fictional characters or real-life people who had to overcome great hardships. Which of these people or events would you like to learn more about? Organize your thoughts before beginning an online search for information.

- Identify the person whom you want to research:
  Answers will vary.

  _____

  _____

  _____

- List the information you want to find about this person:
  Answers will vary.

  _____

  _____

  _____

  _____

- List key words and phrases that you will use in your online search:
  Answers will vary.

  _____

  _____

  _____

After you have completed your online search, answer these questions to help you evaluate your investigation.

- Which words or phrases did you have to change or adjust to find the information you were looking for? Why did they need adjustment?

  Answers will vary.

- Which words or phrases worked best? Why do you think they worked well?

  Answers will vary.

- What tips would you give a friend to help him or her conduct an online search?

  Answers will vary.

UNIT 4 Survival

Planning Investigation

How can you investigate survival further? Write down some ways you can find out more about survival.

Answers will vary.

_____

_____

_____

_____

As you begin your investigation about survival, you will want to keep a list of things you need to do. Check off each item as you complete it. Here is a start of a list of things you might want to remember to do. Add to the list as you become sure about what route your investigation will take.

Things to Do

talk to friends
_____

talk to adults
_____

find and use books from the library
_____

_____

_____

_____

_____

_____

_____

What ideas do you have that you would like to investigate further? Write your thoughts here. If you don't have many ideas right now, that is all right. You will probably think of more ideas as you read the rest of the selections in the unit. Add to this list each time you get a new idea.

Answers will vary.

_____

_____

_____

_____

_____

_____

Now think of ways you can present your information to the rest of the class. You may choose to prepare a poster, a speech, a video, or whatever you think might be the best way to present new information to your classmates. Add to this list as you read and investigate and come up with new ideas.

Answers will vary.

_____

_____

_____

_____

_____

_____

UNIT 4 Survival

Observing and Recording Details

Details make explanations clear and more interesting. Details can include sensory information, such as how something looks, tastes, or sounds, that helps form pictures in the reader's mind.

When recording details, do the following:

• Jot down the important words, phrases, and ideas.
• Do not worry about spelling, punctuation, or grammar.
• Answer as many of these questions as possible: *Who? What? When? Where? Why?* and *How?*

Look at the stories about survival in this unit. Think about how certain characters survived despite misfortune and difficult times. Choose a character from any of the stories. Record the details that vividly show how that character survived.

Character: **Answers will vary.** _____

Details: _____

_____

_____

_____

_____

_____

_____

_____

_____

_____

_____

_____

Think about your investigation. Write the title of your investigation and five details you plan to include in it.

My investigation title is: **Answers will vary.**

1. _____

_____

_____

_____

2. _____

_____

_____

_____

3. _____

_____

_____

_____

4. _____

_____

_____

5. _____

_____

_____

_____

UNIT 4 Survival

Survival Techniques

Throughout the Survival unit, record the different ways that people survive difficult situations. Explain the challenges that the person faced. Think about how you might deal with a similar situation.

Answers will vary.

Conditions   **Survival Techniques**

Conditions   **Survival Techniques**

Conditions

_____
_____
_____
_____
_____

→

Survival Techniques

_____
_____
_____
_____
_____

Conditions

_____
_____
_____
_____
_____

→

Survival Techniques

_____
_____
_____
_____
_____

Conditions

_____
_____
_____
_____
_____

→

Survival Techniques

_____
_____
_____
_____
_____

UNIT 4 Survival

Using Multiple Sources

You have just finished reading "McBroom and the Big Wind." Think of some other topics related to weather about which you would like to learn. Remember, there are many reference sources you can investigate to find information.

- What is something you wonder about?

  Answers will vary.
  _____

  _____

- What library resources could you use to find out more about this subject?

  _____

  _____

- Who could answer your questions about this subject?

  _____

  _____

- What places could you visit to get more information?

  _____

  _____

- How could your wondering make things begin to happen, as in the story?

  _____

  _____

  _____

Making Comparisons

Look at how the characters in the previous selections dealt with survival. In the following boxes, compare the physical and emotional losses each of the characters experienced.

Physical Survival
Story: **Answers will vary.** _____
_____
Situation: _____
_____
_____
Ways of coping: _____
_____
_____

Physical Survival
Story: _____
_____
Situation: _____
_____
_____
Ways of coping: _____
_____
_____

Emotional Survival
Story: _____
_____
Situation: _____
_____
_____
Ways of coping: _____
_____
_____

Emotional Survival
Story: _____
_____
Situation: _____
_____
_____
Ways of coping: _____
_____
_____

Physical Survival

Story: _____

_____

Situation: _____

_____

_____

Ways of coping: _____

_____

_____

Physical Survival

Story: _____

_____

Situation: _____

_____

_____

Ways of coping: _____

_____

_____

Emotional Survival

Story: _____

_____

Situation: _____

_____

_____

Ways of coping: _____

_____

_____

Emotional Survival

Story: _____

_____

Situation: _____

_____

_____

Ways of coping: _____

_____

_____

Map Skills

Map A: The United States Today

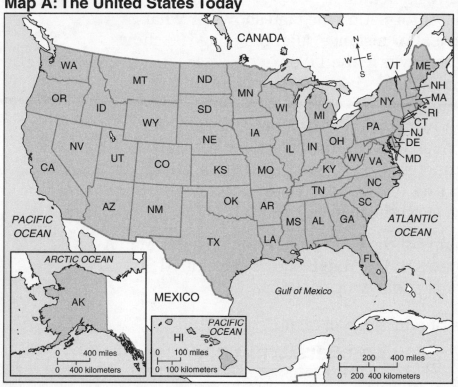

Map B: The United States in the 1780s

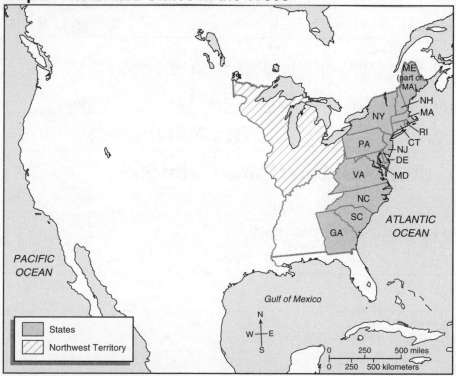

Maps are drawings that show where places or landmarks are located and that have certain features. These include a title, a key, a scale, and a compass rose. Some maps show important and interesting information about the past.

Maps have the following features:

- The **title** tells what information the map shows or what the map's purpose is. For instance, Map B on page 99 shows the United States as it was in the 1780s.
- The **key** tells what each special symbol or color on the map stands for.
- The **scale** shows how many miles or kilometers are represented by a given measure, usually some fraction of an inch or centimeter.
- The **direction arrows** or **compass rose** shows north, south, east, and west on the map.

Look at the two maps of the United States on page 99. Map A shows the United States today. Map B shows the United States in the 1780s. Answer the following questions.

1. What is the name of your state in Map A?

   Write the abbreviation. **Answers will vary.**

2. In Map A, how would you describe the location of your state? (Example: 500 miles west of New York or north of Nebraska)

   Answers will vary.

3. If you are in New Mexico (NM) on Map A, in what direction would you go to get to the Atlantic Ocean? **east**

4. In Map B, what does the map key show? **The Northwest Territory and states in the United States**

How might you use a map in your investigation?

Answers will vary.

Primary and Secondary Sources

Primary sources such as diaries, journals, or newspapers are useful resources for investigation. Secondary sources, or resources that offer background information on a primary source, also aid a researcher in the investigation process. In the boxes below, record examples of primary and secondary sources you have used in your investigation.

Title: **Answers will vary.** _____ Author: _____

Type of primary source: _____

What did you learn from this resource? _____

_____

_____

Title: _____ Author: _____

Type of primary source: _____

What did you learn from this resource? _____

_____

_____

Title: _____ Author: _____

Type of primary source: _____

What did you learn from this resource? _____

_____

_____

Title: **Answers will vary.** _____ Author: _____

Type of secondary source: _____

What did you learn from this resource? _____

_____

_____

Title: _____ Author: _____

Type of secondary source: _____

What did you learn from this resource? _____

_____

_____

Title: _____ Author: _____

Type of secondary source: _____

What did you learn from this resource? _____

_____

_____

Unit Wrap-Up

- How do you feel about this unit?

  ☐ I enjoyed it very much.   ☐ I liked it.

  ☐ I liked some of it.   ☐ I didn't like it.

- How would you rate the difficulty of the unit?

  ☐ easy   ☐ medium   ☐ hard

- How would you rate your performance during this unit?

  ☐ I learned a lot about survival.

  ☐ I learned some new things about survival.

  ☐ I didn't learn much about survival.

- Explain your last answer.

  Answers will vary.

  _____

  _____

  _____

- What was the most interesting thing that you learned about survival?

  Answers will vary.

  _____

  _____

  _____

- What did you learn about survival that you hadn't known before?

  Answers will vary.

- What did you learn about yourself as a learner?

  Answers will vary.

- What do you need to work on as a learner?

  Answers will vary.

- What resources (books, films, magazines, interviews, other) did you use on your own during this unit? Which of these were the most helpful? Why?

  Answers will vary.

Knowledge About Communication

- This is what I know about communication before reading the unit.

  Answers will vary. _____

  _____

  _____

  _____

  _____

  _____

- These are some things I would like to know about communication.

  Answers will vary. _____

  _____

  _____

  _____

  _____

  _____

  Reminder: I should read this page again when I get to the end of the unit to see how much I have learned about communication.

UNIT 5 Communication

Recording Concept Information

As I read each selection, I learned these new facts about communication.

- "Messages by the Mile" by Margery Facklam
  Answers will vary.

_____

_____

_____

_____

_____

_____

_____

- "We'll Be Right Back After These Messages"
  by Shelagh Wallace
  Answers will vary.

_____

_____

_____

_____

_____

_____

_____

- "Breaking into Print" by Stephen Krensky
  Answers will vary.

_____

_____

_____

_____

_____

_____

_____

_____

- "Koko's Kitten" by Dr. Francine Patterson
  Answers will vary.

_____

_____

_____

_____

_____

_____

_____

_____

_____

- "Louis Braille: The Boy Who Invented Books for the Blind"
  by Margaret Davidson
  Answers will vary.

- "My Two Drawings" by Antoine de Saint-Exupéry
  Answers will vary.

Animal Communication

In this unit you will learn about different types of communication in humans and animals. As you think about your investigation, you might want to write about how animals communicate. Much work has been done in the field of animal communication. For instance, researchers have discovered that whales have a unique way of communicating with each other. Look through resources, such as books and magazines, for information about animal communication, and fill in the chart below. Write the type of animal, the names of the researchers, and their findings. Then, think about how you can use this chart in your investigation. You may add to the list as you read additional selections in the unit.

Animal	Researcher(s)	Findings
Answers will vary.		

Project Planning

Use the calendar to help schedule your investigation on Communication. Fill in the dates. Make sure that you mark any days you know you will not be able to work on the project. Then choose the date on which you will start and the date on

Sunday	Monday	Tuesday	Wednesday

which you hope to finish. You may also find it helpful to mark the dates by which you hope to complete each part of the project. Record what you accomplish each day.

Thursday	Friday	Saturday

UNIT 5 Communication

Choosing a Topic

In this unit you will learn about different types of communication in humans and animals. As you think about your investigation, you might want to start by brainstorming ideas about how animals or humans communicate. Once you have a list of ideas, begin formulating questions to help narrow your topic. Look through resources such as books, magazines, or the Internet to help generate questions. Finally, once you have generated questions, rewrite your topic to see how it has changed.

Initial Topic: **Answers will vary.** _____

_____

Question 1: _____

_____

Question 2: _____

_____

Revised Topic: _____

_____

Initial Topic: _____

_____

Question 1: _____

_____

Question 2: _____

_____

Revised Topic: _____

_____

Forming and Revising Questions for Investigation

The selections in this unit contain many possibilities for investigation. Scan the selections and think about how you could further investigate the concept of communication. Write some questions that you would like to investigate further.

Answers will vary.

_____

_____

_____

_____

_____

Choose one of the questions above. Think about how you could revise the question to make it more specific or more interesting. What related questions does this question raise? Write your revised and related questions below.

Answers will vary.

_____

_____

_____

_____

_____

_____

UNIT 5 Communication

Writing About Communication: Review and Feedback

Have a classmate read your investigation to help you improve your writing. Give a classmate your biography, expository writing, or story to read. Write your classmate's name in the space below. Then, give your classmate this page to answer the following questions about your paper. Use a separate sheet of paper if you need more space to write.

Read by (classmate's name): **Answers will vary.** _____

What kinds of communication does the writer report about in the paper?

_____

_____

Is the paper a biography, an expository writing, or a story? How can you tell? Explain here.

_____

_____

Does the writer show what the characters think, feel, say, or do? If not, how can the writer make the characters seem more real?

_____

_____

How can the writer improve the writing in this paper? Answer this question, and write any other suggestions you have for the writer here.

_____

_____

Using Indexes to Find Magazine Articles

Magazine articles are great sources of information for current events and other topics. Choose a topic inspired by "Koko's Kitten," such as American Sign Language, The Gorilla Foundation, Dr. Francine Patterson, gorillas, or animal communication.

Your topic: **Answers will vary.** _____

Two indexes that contain listings of up-to-date magazine articles are the *Reader's Guide to Periodical Literature* and *Children's Magazine Guide*. Go to the library, choose one of these indexes to find two articles listed under your topic, and then fill in the following information.

Magazine index you used: _____

_____

1. Article title: _____

   Author: _____

   Title of magazine: _____

   Date of magazine: _____

   Other sources listed: _____

   _____

   _____

   _____

   _____

   _____

   _____

Summary of article: _____

_____

_____

_____

_____

_____

2. Article title: _____

Author: _____

Title of magazine: _____

Date of magazine: _____

Other sources listed: _____

_____

_____

_____

_____

_____

Summary of article: _____

_____

_____

_____

_____

_____

Biographical Sketch

Look through different sources, such as an encyclopedia or a biographical dictionary, for information about other real-life people who were important to communication. Choose a person and write a short biographical sketch about this person in the box below. Include the important details about why this person was important to communication.

Possible answers shown.

Person: **Alexander Graham Bell**

Biographical sketch: **He is best known for inventing the telephone. The first message spoken into the telephone was, "Mr. Watson, come here. I want you." Bell also invented several techniques for teaching speech to the hearing-impaired.**

Write a short biographical sketch of a classmate in the box below. Include details about where the classmate was born and how they feel about writing.

Person: _____

Biographical sketch: _____

_____

_____

_____

_____

Name _____ Date _____

Developments in Communication

In this unit, you learned about many discoveries in communication through your own reading, investigation, and writing of the investigation. You also learned many interesting facts about communication by asking questions and listening to class presentations by your classmates. Think about the most important facts and discoveries you learned in this unit, and record them in the chart below. Share this information with your classmates. **Possible answers are shown.**

Discoveries or Facts	Reasons That These Discoveries or Facts Are Important
Whales have a language in which they communicate with each other.	**Helps people understand that whales communicate and have a certain level of intelligence.**
Louis Braille invented an easier way for blind people to read and write.	**People who are blind are able to read, write, and communicate more easily using Braille.**

Discoveries or Facts	Reasons That These Discoveries or Facts Are Important

UNIT 5 Communication

Unit Wrap-Up

- How do you feel about this unit?

  ☐ I enjoyed it very much.   ☐ I liked it.

  ☐ I liked some of it.   ☐ I didn't like it.

- How would you rate the difficulty of the unit?

  ☐ easy   ☐ medium   ☐ hard

- How would you rate your performance during this unit?

  ☐ I learned a lot about communication.

  ☐ I learned some new things about communication.

  ☐ I didn't learn much about communication.

- Explain your last answer.
  Answers will vary.
  _____

  _____

  _____

  _____

- What was the most interesting thing that you learned about communication?
  Answers will vary.
  _____

  _____

  _____

  _____

- What did you learn about communication that you hadn't known before?
  Answers will vary.
  _____
  _____
  _____

- What did you learn about yourself as a learner?
  Answers will vary.
  _____
  _____
  _____

- What do you need to work on as a learner?
  Answers will vary.
  _____
  _____
  _____

- What resources (books, films, magazines, interviews, other) did you use on your own during this unit? Which of these were the most helpful? Why?
  Answers will vary.
  _____
  _____
  _____

UNIT 6 A Changing America

Knowledge About A Changing America

- This is what I know about changes in America before reading the unit.

   Answers will vary.

   _____

   _____

   _____

   _____

   _____

- These are some things I would like to know about changes in America.

   Answers will vary.

   _____

   _____

   _____

   _____

   _____

   Reminder: I should read this page again when I get to the end of the unit to see how much I have learned about A Changing America.

Recording Concept Information

As I read each selection, I learned these new facts about changes in America.

- "Early America" by Trevor Matheney
  Answers will vary.
  _____
  _____
  _____
  _____
  _____
  _____
  _____
  _____

- "The Voyage of the Mayflower" by Patricia M. Whalen
  Answers will vary.
  _____
  _____
  _____
  _____
  _____
  _____
  _____
  _____

- "Pocahontas" by Dennis Fradin
  Answers will vary.

  _____

  _____

  _____

  _____

  _____

  _____

  _____

  _____

- "Martha Helps the Rebel" by Carole Charles
  Answers will vary.

  _____

  _____

  _____

  _____

  _____

  _____

  _____

  _____

  _____

- "Going West" by Russell Freedman
  Answers will vary.

_____

_____

_____

_____

_____

- "The California Gold Rush" by Elizabeth Van Steenwyk
  Answers will vary.

_____

_____

_____

_____

_____

- "The Golden Spike" by Dan Elish
  Answers will vary.

_____

_____

_____

_____

_____

Name _____ Date _____

Project Planning

Use the calendar to help schedule your investigation on
A Changing America. Fill in the dates. Make sure that you
mark any days you know you will not be able to work on your
investigation. Then choose the date on which you will start

Sunday	Monday	Tuesday	Wednesday

and the date on which you hope to finish. You may also find it helpful to mark the dates by which you hope to complete different parts of the investigation. Record what you accomplish each day.

Thursday	Friday	Saturday

UNIT 6 A Changing America

Settlers in the New World

The settlers who came to the New World faced many problems and hardships. As you read the selections in this unit, write who the settlers were, the problems they faced, and how they solved the problems. Then, think about how you might use this information for your investigation.

Settlers	Problems	Solutions
The colonists in the Jamestown colony	Disease and starvation	They learned how to adapt to a new land. They received some help from Native Americans.
The Pilgrims	Crowded and uncomfortable conditions on the *Mayflower*	They cooperated with each other when cooking meals and doing chores.

Settlers	Problems	Solutions

UNIT 6 A Changing America

Conjecture Phase

Our problem:

Answers will vary.

_____

_____

_____

_____

_____

_____

Conjecture (my first theory or explanation):

_____

_____

_____

_____

_____

_____

_____

_____

As you collect information, your conjecture will change. Return to this page to record your new theories or explanations about your investigation.

Choosing a Topic

In this unit, you will learn about the people, places, and important events in A Changing America. Think about a topic you would like to write about for your investigation. You might investigate a particular colony in the New World or compose a fictional travel brochure of your own state. You might also imagine yourself as an explorer and write a diary of your life in a young America.

- Write your ideas about a topic you might like to investigate.

Answers will vary.

_____

_____

_____

_____

_____

_____

- What information do you need to help you figure out how to begin your investigation? For instance, do you need to know the name and location of a particular colony? Write your ideas or questions here.

_____

_____

_____

_____

_____

_____

UNIT 6 A Changing America

Plays

A play is a story that is performed in front of an audience. The story is told through dialogue and the actions of the characters. *Martha Helps the Rebel* is a play that brings to life scenes from colonial America. Think about a play you might like to write about a colonial or early American event, situation, or person. Write the title and cast of characters in the space below. Then write the setting and three scenes. Write dialogue and stage directions that make your characters come to life. Use a separate sheet of paper if you need more room to write.

Title: **Answers will vary.** _____

Cast of Characters: _____

_____

_____

_____

Setting: _____

_____

_____

_____

Scene One: _____

_____

_____

_____

_____

_____

_____

Scene Two: _____

_____

_____

_____

_____

_____

_____

_____

Scene Three: _____

_____

_____

_____

_____

_____

_____

_____

_____

_____

UNIT 6 A Changing America

Using the Card or Computer Catalog

The card or computer catalog lists all the books a library has. The catalog can be found in the library's computer or on cards in a file cabinet with small drawers. Look at the sample card below.

DICK WHITTINGTON

J
398.22
STO   Storr, Catherine.
Dick Whittington/retold by Catherine Storr; illustrated by Jane Bottomly.—Milwaukee: Raintree Children's Books, ©1986.
[32] p.: col. ill.; 25 cm.
Summary: Retells the traditional tale of the poor boy in medieval England who became Lord Mayor of London.
1. Whittington, Richard, d. 1423
2. Folklore—England.

Here is a list of information found on cards in a card catalog.
- There are three types of cards: **author**, **title**, and **subject** cards. Depending on the type of card, either the author's name, the title of the book, or the subject will be at the top of the card. For instance, the title appears at the top of a title card.
- The call number is in the upper left corner of every card. This number matches the numbers and letters on the spine of the book. This number tells you where to find the book in the library.
- Every card lists the year the book was published and the name and location of the publisher, the number of pages, the abbreviation *ill.* if the book has illustrations, and the size of the book.
- The card includes a brief summary of what the book is about.
- At the bottom of each card is a list that shows all the headings the book is listed under in the card catalog.

Find two books you might use for investigation. Record the information you find in the card catalog on the blank cards below. Make sure you copy the information as it appears on the cards.

Answers will vary.

UNIT 6 A Changing America

Using Museums to Get Information

Museums are helpful resources when you are investigating. If your area has a museum that might help you in your investigation, visit it and share with your classmates the information you find there. If no museum is available, complete the questions below about the usefulness of museums in general. **Answers will vary.**

What types of information do museums contain? _____

_____

_____

_____

What might you learn at a museum? _____

_____

_____

_____

How might that information help you with your investigation?

_____

_____

_____

Find the name of a museum (in a library catalog or another resource) that you might contact to help in your investigation.

_____

_____

_____

Assessing Your Resources

As you work on your investigation, try to gather as many different resources as you can. Look through the information you have already gathered for your investigation. Did you get most of your information from one kind of resource? If most of your resources are the same, think about other resources you can use for your topic. Use the chart below to check the different resources you might use.

Source	Useful?	How?
Encyclopedias		**Answers will vary.**
Books		
Magazines		
Newspapers		
Videotapes, filmstrips, etc.		
Television		
Interviews, observations		
Museums		
Other		

UNIT 6 A Changing America

Verifying Sources

List four facts from "The California Gold Rush." List the
sources you might use to verify each fact.

Atlas: a book containing many maps
Almanac: a book containing up-to-date facts, published each year
Encyclopedia: a set of books with information on many topics,
arranged in alphabetical order
Biographical dictionary: a dictionary containing facts about famous
people
Geographical dictionary: a dictionary containing facts about places
in the world

Fact: **Answers will vary.** _____

_____

Sources: _____

Fact: _____

_____

Sources: _____

Fact: _____

_____

Sources: _____

Fact: _____

_____

Sources: _____

Drawing Conclusions from Information

Drawing conclusions from the information you find for your investigation will help you learn as you read and write. You draw conclusions by carefully reading the details and facts in the material you are reading. The conclusion may not be stated but should be supported by examples from the text.

Read the information below about sea mammals.

Whales, dolphins, manatees, seals, sea lions, and sea otters are marine mammals. Marine mammals spend most of their time underwater, but must come to the surface to breathe. Whales were once hunted for their blubber, oil, and bones. Seals and sea otters were hunted for their fur. Today, most nations have laws protecting marine mammals.

• What conclusions about marine mammals can you make after reading the paragraph? Use the information above to draw conclusions about sea mammals.

Answers will vary but may include that marine mammals are or are becoming endangered.

_____

_____

_____

_____

_____

_____

_____

Drawing Conclusions from Information *(continued)*

Choose another topic you might use for your investigation.
Select a source, such as an encyclopedia, dictionary, or almanac,
to find information about your topic. Write your topic title,
your source, and the information you found on your topic.

Topic title: **Answers will vary.** _____

Source: _____

- Write a brief summary of the information here.

_____
_____
_____
_____
_____
_____
_____

- Draw conclusions using the information you found about
  your topic.

_____
_____
_____
_____
_____
_____
_____

Comparing Information

"Going West," "The California Gold Rush," and "The Golden Spike" are excerpts from longer books. Reread the excerpts in the student anthology. Think about the information in each selection. Then, answer the questions below.

- How are the excerpts alike?
  Answers will vary.
  _____
  _____
  _____
  _____

- How are the excerpts different?
  Answers will vary.
  _____
  _____
  _____
  _____

- Which source or sources provides a detailed account of life in the Old West? **Possible answers are shown.**
  Going West, California Gold Rush

- Which source or sources would you use to find out why people emigrated to the West?
  Going West, California Gold Rush

- Which source or sources would you use to learn about the growth of America?
  Going West, The Golden Spike

UNIT 6 A Changing America

Unit Wrap-Up

- How do you feel about this unit?

  ☐ I enjoyed it very much.   ☐ I liked it.

  ☐ I liked some of it.   ☐ I didn't like it.

- How would you rate the difficulty of the unit?

  ☐ easy   ☐ medium   ☐ hard

- How would you rate your performance during this unit?

  ☐ I learned a lot about A Changing America.

  ☐ I learned some new things about A Changing America.

  ☐ I didn't learn much about A Changing America.

- Explain your last answer.

  Answers will vary.

  _____

  _____

  _____

  _____

- What was the most interesting thing that you learned
  about A Changing America?

  Answers will vary.

  _____

  _____

  _____

  _____

- What did you learn about A Changing America that you hadn't known before?

   Answers will vary.

- What did you learn about yourself as a learner?

   Answers will vary.

- What do you need to work on as a learner?

   Answers will vary.

- What resources (books, films, magazines, interviews, other) did you use on your own during this unit? Which of these were the most helpful? Why?

   Answers will vary.